Spirit Unchained

Collected Poems, 1967-2014

Spirit Unchained:
The Autobiography of a Soul

Collected Poems, 1967-2014

by
James B. Moore

edited by
Phil Bevis & Geoff Wallace

Chatwin Books
SEATTLE, 2015

Poems and afterword copyright the author, 2000-2015

Edited by Phil Bevis and Geoff Wallace, with the assistance of Gregg Andrews. This Chatwin publication is powered by Booktrope. Cover design by Annie Brulé. Book design by Phil Bevis and Annie Brulé. Editorial and design content copyright Chatwin Books, 2015. All rights reserved.

Visit us on the web at www.ChatwinBooks.com

ISBN 978-1-63398-001-3 (paperback)
ISBN 978-1-63398-030-3 (hardcover)

to Esther

foreword

You are about to meet a man by reading over forty years of his writings. In many ways, it is neither an easy introduction nor a comfortable journey. You will not be meeting the man as the person he is—you will be experiencing his process of becoming.

The poems begin in the author's early youth, with strong narratives that recount an inherited persona of streetwise toughness. Some of these early poems define, some bruise, some shock. In their wake we find a boy taking his first puzzled steps toward manhood, carrying with him— almost without question—the legacy of a rough family layered with scar tissue from surviving street and dystopian surroundings.

Following this chapter are the perspectives and experiences of late teenage years, college, military, life as a merchant seaman, professional musician, teacher, and as a single man. Each epoch is marked by often-painful collisions with others, whether they be rough-edged men or, all too frequently, the women the poet always needs but never seems to understand.

At some point, age brings with it an appreciation for the essence of life and the part of human identity that exists beyond the tactile. The wisdom of this transformation is followed by a very different body of work—deeper and sometimes mystical in its meditation—a work of contemplation, acceptance, and an approach to inner peace.

Seeing this book as the story of a poet, or of a man, would miss much of the work's meaning. It is more than a collection of poems, more than a life. What we have in *Spirit Unchained* is the autobiography of a soul.

Phil Bevis, Seattle, October 2014

table of contents

foreword	page 7
part I - rough start	11
part II - diving into shallow waters	53
part III - uneven path	95
part IV - breaking the surface	131
part V - fresh dawn	165
part VI - toward the horizon	187
author's afterword	205
index of poems by title	209

part I - rough start

unchained spirit

he
was one tough son of a bitch
born hot-blooded Gypsy
mother died when he was four
father left him drifting
house to house on Boston streets

his first day of school
a child jammed a pencil
up a little girl's nose
this blamed unwanted orphan
with no one to defend him
was locked overnight
in a second story classroom
while strangers sealed his fate

escaping down a drainpipe
he chose a different education
the world of child labor sweatshops
beaten for playing on the job
he grew to understand his bondage
learned to think about survival
as freedom on the streets

at nineteen he chose a bride
fresh off a Polish cattle boat
a greenhorn needing his protection
tailor-made to worship John
he left the streets to start a family
worked as hotel elevator boy

a pimp there tried to strangle John
who wouldn't do as he was told
in self defense he taught the pimp to fly

head first down an elevator shaft
moved his family to Chicago
changed his name to beat the heat

five-foot-four
one hundred fifteen pounds
John moved pianos
played fiddle in bars
bought high grade alcohol
from Al Capone
doctored it
sent my mother out at ten
in oversized coats
containing hidden inside pockets
delivering booze to speakeasies
where she was affectionately greeted
as John's daughter

leaving a bar late one night
jumped by four men
he walked thirty blocks
knife to hilt in neck
pulled it out, doctored the wound
stayed in bed two weeks
returned to waste the knifer
kept a jeweled gold pocket watch
to celebrate his victory

later middle-aged John retired from Chicago streets
found a secluded country farm
bought half-dead nags
paid five dollars each
doctored them
sold healthy horses for fifty more

born while dad was called away to World War Two
my early years were spent
with John
my first steps, first words
were with John
I'd hang laughing
from his ear lobes
while the family stared
in horror
knowing well his fiery temper
John just chuckled

tumbling down a flight of stairs
teeth ripped through my tongue
which hung by shreds of skin
knowing the country doctor
as morphine addict
whose stitch of tongue would
leave a lisp
John bonded it together
left not stitch or lisp

when dad again was sent
to Korea
we lived behind a
country grocery store
John made me ice cream cones
ignoring sounds of dinner waiting
he'd let me leave my
bed at night
sit at his feet and listen
as cronies from primal streets
shared soldiers' tales of prohibition

John fiercely loved me
and I loved him
his Gypsy blood rushed
howling through my veins

when Dad returned
John was dying
walking growling through his day
no measurable pulse
cancerous hole in throat
not ready to go

a large angry man
entered the store
demanding exchange
for a child's half eaten candy bar
John refused
the man grew mean
Dad arrived in time
to hold the door open
while John grabbed him
by his shirt and
seat of his pants
tossing the disbelieving bully
three feet into the road

I have not since seen
such unconquerable spirit
this courageous exercise
of will over body

John died shortly after
leaving the gold watch
brass knuckles
a blackjack

other more traditional inheritances
and a message
"to be anything you goddamn want!"

he danced an extraordinary dance
then passed it on
to me

may i see wandell, please

at seven
I adored Dad
walked like him
talked like him
would do anything
to make him proud
a quiet man
he kept to himself
I only heard through Mother
about his wild youth
boxing title
military fame
decorations for valor
the respect people gave him

avoiding the spotlight
he preferred reading books
playing harmonica
strumming his ukulele
singing with us at night
he'd pat Mom
playfully from behind
thinking I wouldn't see
often he sat alone
looking sad
remembering the war, Mom said
that part of him I never knew
but I knew
he'd never let me down

one hot summer day
running home crying
clothes torn

lip bleeding
I found Dad
sitting on the front porch
drinking a cold beer
"What's the matter, kid?"
"Wandell beat me up."
"What'd you let him
do that for?"
"He's bigger'n me
and three years older," I sobbed
trying to hold back
the humiliation
"Well, pick up a stick then."
"Okay Dad," I said
slowly leaving for Wandell's house

passing a vacant lot
I picked up a two-by-four
proceeding with shaking knees
to knock on Wandell's door
his father—the town police chief
opened the door
observing my bloody lip
torn clothes
tear stained cheeks
board on shoulder
asked, "What can I do
for you?"
"May I see Wandell, please?" I stammered
eyes softening, he quietly said
"Not now son, he's busy."

returning home, Dad was
hanging up the phone
eyes twinkling

"Wandell's dad said he
 couldn't come out," I whispered
 his voice was tender
"It's okay, kid."

damn yankee

"damn yankee, damn yankee"
on my first day of school
in a small southern town
my northern accent
targeted me as different

the civil war
was not yet over
in 1950
several boys shoved me
knocked me down

one grabbed my lunch box
I tried to grab it back
he tossed it to the first boy
I tackled him

he laughed and sneered
as I began to even the score
his nose began to bleed
adults appeared, pulling me off

jerking loose
again jumping the bully
I was determined
to finish my business

someone found my mother
who dragged me off
demanding that I
apologize

I refused
she apologized to everyone
took me by the ear

refused to hear
my explanation

headed for home
sent me to my room
where I was left
waiting
"till your father gets home"

after dark

in a small Louisiana town
in 1950
black men were considered
dangerous after dark
to white women
who were protected
by forcing black men
to keep their place
across the town line
by sundown, 8pm sharp

a curious seven-year-old
newly arrived from Chicago
pretended to nap
crept out the bedroom window
drawn toward angry noises
from a mob
chasing a shrieking boy
about fifteen
and five minutes late
getting across the line

someone tackled him
held him down
fear silenced the boy
as the crowd began
to beat him, beat him

they drenched his body
with steaming hot tar
his brown skin
dissolved into bloody pink
was shrouded in feathers

his body flung
onto a passing freight

the air hung heavy
with pungently sweet stench
the little boy gagged
ran home leapt through the bedroom window
melted into bed
trying to disappear
his mother opened the door
"Dinner's ready."
"Not hungry, Mommy."
"Okay, honey. Maybe later,"
 she said, gently closing the door

train ride

gazing out of the window
of a decaying northbound train
a frowning nine-year-old
remembers his father's words
spoken from a hospital bed
"Take care of your mother, son,
until I get home. You're
the man of the house now."
the boy pushes back his fear
of missing his stop
losing Grandma's luggage
no one at the station to meet them

with a trusting smile
his mentally slow grandma
knows she's returning home safely
from her daughter's surgery
to her cancer-ridden John

staring at the landscape
fixed on his task
shaking off a cold chill
the boy listens
through blurring fields
listens past fading towns
for the conductor's call
"Michigan City, next stop!"

the code

ten years old
on the south side of Chicago
in a tough neighborhood
a local hood
confronted me, demanding money

I jumped him
fighting hard
we tumbled onto the sidewalk
rolling into the gutter
children and adults gathered

he grabbed my throat
choking me
my fists pummeled his stomach
hard and fast as I could
people began betting

face turning blue
I couldn't breathe
blood hemorrhaged
out his mouth
spattering our shirts

walking to the grocery store
my mother saw us
screamed to stop
"Keep out of it, Mom," I gasped
she froze watching

still pounding his stomach
I began to lose consciousness
he groaned
released my throat
gargled through his blood, "I quit."

gasping for air
struggling to my feet
I slowly staggered away
Mother quietly resumed her shopping
the crowd settled their bets

the new kid

twelve years old
my first day of school
in Seattle
I approached the school gorilla
determined to cut my losses
and only get creamed once
in Chicago
a new kid had to fight his way
up through the pecking order
to make his place

there he was, King Kong
wide as he was tall
solid muscle
future golden gloves boxer
dark menacing look
I called him out
he slowly turned
looking amazed he asked
"Who are you?
What planet are you from?"
I growled my answer
bracing for his charge

he whispered almost tenderly
"You don't want to fight me—
I could kill you."
proceeding to introduce me
to two speechless boys
"This is Jim from Chicago.
Let's show him the ropes
before he gets busted."
grinning, he extended his paw
Seattle was, indeed
another planet

performance cancelled

as high school was ending
I was just beginning
as singer songwriter musician
performing at school assemblies
beach parties, small clubs
singing and strumming my banjo
formed a bridge
between my shyness and the world
half of me hid behind the
performance
the other half danced my dreams

my friend Tom
asked if I would play
a party for his family
I found myself surrounded
by older worldly actors
from a local theater group
as I played and sang
a friendly hand caressed my leg
a sexy twenty-three-year old
decided she wanted my
virginity
which was all right with me

the party grew wilder
Tom's parents passed out
I called home
"Tom's parents asked if I
 could spend the night."
the phone grew silent
then my father's voice boomed
"Get your ass home!"

fear of my father's hand
loomed larger than what was stirring
toward the hand
moving up my leg
I left

ten years later I asked dad
if he remembered that night
"Did you know
you kept me from
losing my virginity?"
he laughed
"Why do you think I told you
to get your ass home."

is that all

I was seventeen
a freshman at the university
dating a lovely twenty-year-old
I had met at a party
at first she was attracted
to my playing and singing
later she was drawn
to my youthful innocence

the way she touched me
looked into my eyes
purred when I touched her
released a tenderness
and a primal scream
I didn't know I had

one night I told her
"We need to break up."
her eyes widened with surprise
"Why?"
"Because I want you so badly
I'm afraid I won't . . .
won't be able
to control myself."
with a relieved sigh
she said "Is that all."

the next night
I borrowed a friend's car
drove to a secluded park
we began
petting, kissing, undressing
she smiled, drifted back
gently pulled me down

helped me ease inside
it was a lovely velvet ride
lasting at least
eight seconds
I came

confused, embarrassed
I looked into her eyes helplessly
"This is your first time, isn't it."
I nodded yes
she touched my face
tenderly kissed my lips
"Honey, you'll be
a wonderful lover.
I'll teach you."

and she did

hanging down

Sunday morning, 1962
my girlfriend's parents are
walking me to the car

neighbors stroll by
smiling, nodding hello
on their way to church

suddenly
I spot a used Trojan
glued to the side of the car
last night's banner limply waving

quickly grabbing it
I cram it into my pocket
forcing a smile
as my girlfriend's mother
lovingly hugs me goodbye

the road most traveled

at swim practice
a college freshman
swimming hard as he could
finished last
pushing himself to the limit
almost catching the other swimmers
on the last lap

"Swim another lap!" the coach ordered
wanting to see if he was holding back
the boy barely finished the lap
was too exhausted
to pull himself out of the pool

afterward in the locker room
knowing of the youth's passionate involvement
with his first love
the coach quietly approached the boy
"You've got to choose
between swimming and women,
you can't do both."
the youth frowned
"Then I'll have to leave, coach."

walking out of the locker room
the boy breathed a sigh of relief
his pain was over
he couldn't have quit
on his own
the coach watched him go
smiling knowingly
rubbing his crotch

clarence

rolling the dice
my ninth straight pass
in a seedy hotel room
over a whorehouse bar
in Ketchikan, Alaska

surrounded by growling merchant seamen
who become more surly
each time I make my point
I shoot a seven and smile

someone yells "Son of a bitch!"
grabs the dice, examines them
slowly shakes his head
slams them back down

Clarence stands behind me
my only friend in the room
emaciated, white haired, sixty-one
a sweet and kindly man
he doesn't talk much

spends his shore time getting
staggering drunk
on board ship Clarence
teaches me seaman's skills

I look out for him on shore
the man needs a friend
he could be me at
his age after a few bad breaks
but I'm nineteen
tonight, king of the hill

I throw an eleven
someone smashes a bottle against the wall
"I'm leaving," I nervously announce
two men block the door
one of them flashes a knife
"Not with all our money you
won't, motherfucker," he sneers

Clarence steps between us
flicks his switchblade
the room grows quiet
no one is challenging him
there's a side of Clarence I do not know
"Let me handle this, Jim," he quietly cautions

they agree to let me throw five more passes
buy them several cases of beer
then I may leave
slowly shaking the dice
concentrating on losing
I reluctantly continue to win
all five passes

Clarence motions to leave
backs out behind me, knife circling
we walk downstairs, order the beer
I try to thank Clarence
attempt to give him half the money
he gently waves it away

"I don't want your money.
I'd just drink it up.
Listen, son, when the beer is gone, they'll
come for you.
You've won enough to go back to school,"
he looks away

"to make something of your life.
Don't end up like me."

an hour later I board
the red-eye flight to Seattle
Clarence hugs me, says goodbye
tears welling in his eyes
unable to speak, I turn
board the plane

male bonding

strumming my banjo and singing
at my last high school beach party
someone offers me a drink
from the communal bottle of Thunderbird wine

a voice booms across the beach
"I hate banjos!"
our all-state center, Dick Hard
yes, Dick Hard
one day to join the L.A. Rams
the missing link
270 pounds of steaming shit
drunkenly staggers towards me
screaming "I hate banjo players!"

people try to stop him
he scatters bodies like cordwood
shuffles to an unsteady halt
directly in front of me
I hold my banjo like a club
knowing I have just one shot
then I'm hamburger

Dick looks down at me
sees something
smiles, winks
then staggers away
leaving me, mouth open
reaching for the Thunderbird

two years later
at a Carmel, California bar
after performing at a local club
well into a bottle of vodka

the man to my right
draws a picture on a bar napkin
of a hand with middle finger extended
hands it to the bartender
tells him to deliver it
to a surly looking giant
seated at the end of the bar

he growls "Who drew this?"
the man to my right points at me
shaking off a cold chill
I try to get up off the barstool
find I can't stand
sit back down helplessly

the giant stomps over
puts a hairy arm around my neck
while the man to my right
the man to my left
the bartender
everyone at the bar
explodes into laughter
I am being welcomed

smiling weakly I accept
several free drinks
thinking to myself
"I never really did understand
 male bonding."

the hunt

one weekend a friend
talked me into hunting deer
not having the stomach
to kill a helpless animal
I decided to go
to see what would happen

my friend and I separated
each taking a hill
at the bottom of mine
stood a young buck, alert and beautiful
I could not pull the trigger

hearing a rustle in the brush
I turned to see another hunter,
quietly concealed, aiming at me
"Hey, I am not a deer!"
the buck disappeared over the hill
he continued drawing a bead

I crouched, drawing him into my sights
"If you don't leave I'll shoot."
he disappeared
a shot crackled over the hill
my friend shot the deer

the next week I read in the paper
of a man that had been killed, 'a hunting accident'
the shooter remained unidentified
my friend and I chewed on deer steak,
badly dressed and bitter
I never went hunting again

the chosen

there were
two of us
chosen
to spice up the English department
at one of the top ten
high schools
in the country
we had come to join a select few
to make the curriculum
more relevant
to the counterculture revolution
of 1967

Spencer had recently published
a social protest novel
I was a folk-rock performer
who wrote poetry
we had come to join
a humanistic alliance
dedicated to teaching how,
not what, to think

the department chairman
old Bill Lamont
created a humanities program
that received national recognition
his kind gentle urbane ways
sometimes sparkled with passion
which could flicker or stream
he drank his wine from the bottle
played guitar and sang with us
at our welcoming party

attending our first department meeting
we sat expectantly
the meeting began
one by one they
attacked Bill
personally, professionally
complained about a lack
of student respect
owed them
regardless of how they taught
running out of complaints
they bickered with one another

I sat depressed
Spencer
threw up in the bathroom
as we left
Bill joined us in the hall
put an arm around each of us
and said
"They labored
and labored
giving birth
to a fart."

to whom it may concern

O teacher who art in heaven
hallowed be thy truth
revise
   criticize
      christianize
castrate the mind
the blood will dry
and coagulate to your design

army reserve summer camp '68

here I sit at Fort Ord
watching forty men becoming clerical machines
four weeks of mental automation
as the system perpetuates itself

I hope it doesn't dwarf them
it shouldn't though
at least not more
than some teachers I know

micelike

   micelike
heading towards the sea
   like lemmings
driving
   ravaging nature
rushing
   crying loneliness
whoa
   who the fucks idea was this!

five minutes

at one o'clock in the morning
man emerged a thinking being
with a god created in his image
an all-important thinking being

but a violence persisted
and man was forced to make
ritualistic-like excuses
to explain his fall from grace

the development continued
until the present day arrived
we're so much more advanced now
today it's 1:05.

make it noisy

meeting a skater
after an Ice Capades performance
her partner hugs us both
says "You two have fun
but don't feed her.
I have to lift her in the morning."

the day before she'd brought me home
introducing me to her
pretentious socialite parents
their chilly reception reflecting
a teacher's lower economic status

impatiently she grabs my
hand leads me to her
bedroom pulls me down and
purrs "make it noisy."

back again

a young and stoned musician
drifted from his band
playing football on the beach,
to ride off-limits waves

smashed his head against the surfboard
saw his double under water
swirled into glowing timewarp
ah, the all-consuming love
he knew but had forgotten
an overwhelming coming home

a loving murmur whispered gently
you must go back, you are not done
awakening on the beach
he took a swing at the lifeguard

the caress

he caressed his guitar
spraying blues across the strings
smiled as he fondled the box
and whispered
"You've got something to say tonight, boy.
Get your voice,"
and he plugged in
the amplifier

simple wisdom

a young man
visits a small town
to meet an old man
a great one
finds him
in an outdoor cafe
turns to a waiter
asks about him

"He's lived here all his life,"
says the waiter
the old man observes the youth
nods towards a chair

as they talk
his simple wisdom
touches the youth
"Why have you remained here
all your life?"
"I haven't," smiled the old man,
"not yet."

snakes know

I read
local rattlesnakes
rattle their warning
when large animals
come too close
but they seldom
bite

humans learned
to follow the
sound
and kill
for the fun of it

rattlers learned
not to
rattle at people
reserving
the silent strike
for the most deserving

scratch

a withered, lonely wisp of a tree
leans against a weathered brick building
it pounds and scratches as if it had fists
one could say it's just the wind, but
if you listen you can hear it mutter indignantly

the tree must know it can never win
why does it struggle so
maybe it's heard of its redwood cousin
who endures until nature's disruptions pass
or maybe it knows the winning is not so important
it's the scratching that counts

part II - diving into shallow waters

now

now is pretty
spattered with lacelike pleasure
intertwining smiles
quiet satisfaction
pleasingly drifting in
now is you

let me

let me
ease inside your wonder
move my tongue into your thunder
ride you madly into midnight
touch you deeply with my dreams' light

then I will know that it was worth
the screaming struggle
for my birth

my lady

my lady stretches across her bed
and her ass is a marvelous thing
pink and heart-shaped, shining like the sun
she smiles and beckons, her heart even finer
warming me from the cold night air

I watch her butt, her pink, tight, magic butt
it raises my spirits like fine Spanish wine
and she is mine
she catches the light of the sun and laughs back at me
a woman among little girls, singing take me if you dare

we make pink, red, white hot love
never ending, moving, drifting
in and out of each other's souls
flying, racing, slowly languishing
timelessly letting go of all struggle
flowing so deeply into each other that
orgasm becomes anticlimax

we lie intertwined
having no desire to let go or move away, or sleep
in awe of the joy we feel as we touch
vagina and penis becoming interchangeable
our love so large our bodies cannot contain it

it flows around our bodies
filling the room, oozing down the hall
cascading over stairs, pouring out doors and windows
our loving changes doors and windows into sunlight
her tight, silken embrace moves me to laughter, to tears
and time stands still as our souls fall into one-another

the gentle wind whispers

as I try to imagine
living my life without you
you suddenly appear
for only a moment
scattering my contentment
as I drift into thoughts of you

I walk the streets at night
remembering tender moments
in an old Spanish hotel
when for a brief time
time and your leaving
was suspended

your smile is reflected
in the light of street lamps
it shimmers on mud puddles
as the gentle wind whispers
I love you
I love you

only the wind knows the future
tonight I embrace the wind
it is all I have of you
as I continue on alone
feeling your presence in every moment

moonlight ride

lost in long forgotten heartaches
in the shadow of a memory
that had drifted into darkness
reawakened by the teardrops
that are cutting through a half-smile
streams a pathway through the evening
with a bittersweet reflection
about the sadness in a lifetime

crying we have never done
will penetrate the moonlight
with a need for something more
in the shelter of a bottle
laced with traces of a memory
graying shadows in the rain
that whisper to me softly
not to take this path again

feelings boiling in the background
coffee blacker than a coal mine
primal chords so deep within me
meeting edges of the night
o' bitch of all-consuming anguish
kiss my muse and touch my mind
straddle daydreams like a harlot
without a caring for my soul

fucking me with screaming sorrow
with no feeling for the loving
tearing at my very core
seeping into rays of daylight
as the brightness makes it stop
again I hang there slowly waiting
for the night to overcome me
to ride the darkness once again

fuck and die

fuck me
make like a garbage truck
or a poet

welcoming anything
pumping downhill
without any brakes

bubonic orgasm
shooting out my penis
dripping out your vagina

pulling me
into everyone you've ever had
injecting you
with everyone I've ever had

leaving us bleeding
from every pore
disease tonguing our assholes
we can't miss

interrupted journey

a road-weary traveler met a charming hitchhiker
caught in the lanes of her freeway

he parked his dreams at the curb of her mouth
and fear lined her throat

he revealed the space between her chain links
and she welded it shut

he dispelled her illusion of guru's robes
and she saw only a man

he offered his depth
and she ran from the abyss

he left in pained silence
as she sighed in relief

swan dive

I'm doing a slow motion
swan dive off the top stair
landing twisted at the bottom
with the sound of cracking ribs

around the corner in the
kitchen my wife is doing
something
has no response to the crash
groaning I say
"I'm driving to emergency—
think I've hurt my back."
"Okay" is all she says

waiting at the hospital
I realize our marriage
is over

she

she became unreachable
her soul fled

arms outstretched
I tried to grasp it, put it back

failing
was left to tend to my own

princess leaping

starting out
pampered ivory princess
cultivating the look
not word or hair
out of place
smiling on command

she searched
for at least one wealthy man
focusing pussy trimmed attention
around smoothly crafted moves
few knew the difference
even she forgot

losing her direction
and other tighter
assets
she closed her tearless eyes
and lept
into a frozen blowjob sky

cinderella and the seven dwarfs

slipping her body over many lovers
anxiously seeking
the right fit

destroying her body
and a few lovers

she grew bitter
cause she forgot
to slip on
her soul

reflections from the hungry turtle cocktail lounge

hoarse whispers
freshly spilled bourbon melting into cigarette breath
the sound of Ray Stevens singing everything is beautiful

red panties through white jeans
varicose veins crawling up newly fattened legs
once-flat stomach
sturdy knowing thighs

tired, bleary-eyed businessmen
tenderly caressing their glasses
rubbing their eyes at the bar
flirting with their imagination

don't you kill him

at a nightclub
after midnight
on New Year's Eve
with a beautiful, much younger
woman

we leave arm in arm, smiling
a hooker at the next table
calls out to my date
"Don't you kill him tonight, girl!"

as we both laugh
I notice my date's laughter
is louder

bimbo love

"well, I was kind of
not enthralled with
him
ummm
and
by the end of the evening
I got thralled."

the light bled

a moan-a-lisa smile
wrapped around her unawakened soul
exiting out her mouth
which puckered like a flesh wound

clawlike on my leg
skeletal fingers
squeezed and gashed my genitals

even the light bled
trickling onto my unhinged jaw
a crooked result
of one blow too many

pouring into weary eyes
blurred and squinted
from the throwing of acid

oozing into muted ears
edges blurred
from playing guitar too close to speakers

a punchy fighter
reeling with angst
scar tissue inside and out

jagged with romance and other life struggles
screaming
demanding his due

bye

you casually leave
and tell me
that you love me
but we have
irreconcilable differences
of course, that's not open
for discussion

you say
let's be friends
you don't get
my friendship
baby
you get
a tired goodbye

deep

you're in deep shit now
  she said
I hope so
   I said
I've been looking for deep shit all my life

the gift

I called her late at night
after a year
"I want to see you."
"Now?" she said. "I'm in bed."
"I know," I said, "yes, now
just say yes and I'm on my way."

"Yes."

it was a long drive
there was no moon
only the lights of others, riding the freeway
on some hopeless task or other

I arrived
she was fully dressed, drinking wine, distant
"I'm seeing someone," she said.
"Who?"
she told me
"There's no formal commitment yet. Do you know him?"
"Yes—he's manipulative."
"I think he's nice," she said.
"You'll see."
"What are you doing?" she asked.
"I'm leaving."

on the long drive home I thought about the conversation
and her coldness
with a deep sense of relief I realized
I had been given a gift

do you love her you poor bastard

do you love her
the way I loved her
expecting nothing
because she was changing

she'll leave you too
you know

her changes
leveraged to keep distance
avoid vulnerability
each shared
with someone new

as you wait
in vain
for her to heal
she creates separate lives
sharing one with you
others conceal clandestine adventures
never to be integrated

there is you
there are others
there is her
her

her

her

up

I've upped my priorities
baby
up yours

crystal snifter

passing out
four brandy snifters
she looks at me
and says
"That's yours, isn't it."

I smile
passing my crystal snifter
and say
"Let me have a sip
and it's yours."

she nods yes
I sip
the aged German nectar
my fingers exploring
the crystal prisms
encircling the base

savoring the uneven roughness
tickling the bottom of the glass
inching upward
fondling tear-like indentions
that beckon
toward my lips

a gently sculpted upward motion
opens
like a budding rose
shamelessly
offering its precious contents

princess bride

a true princess never discusses
financial details of her wedding
such distasteful tasks are left
to mother
who manipulates everyone

a princess, recognizing this
would have to face mother
manipulating her
training her to scheme in turn
to believe she is justified to judge
anyone who questions what a
princess thinks

there's a recipe for cooking up
a well-seasoned princess
first add a cup of emotional distance
toward her father
who long ago left princess mom
for being emotionally unavailable

then add one young man
who truly loves princess bride
following a code of his own
to honor, cherish, and not make
too many demands

one day loneliness will
contradict his code
placing him on collision's course
crotch first into the pedestal
upon which princess sits

sharing his deepest feelings
her cold response drives the youth to

cloak his loneliness in charade
until he comes to understand
she will never be his partner
leaving him to seek a woman who
does not subscribe to princess codes

mom and princess both conclude
he simply wasn't good enough
as they indoctrinate their daughter
the fledgling princess bride

shifted

over time
my attitude towards women
shifted

in youth
I passionately promised
"I won't hurt you"

later
I found myself pleading
"please don't hurt me"

men are like dogs

one smiling morning
while leaving your house
I left behind
a black polo shirt
maybe in a bundle on your closet floor
or hanging somewhere
kind of like a dog peeing on a tree
a primal fingerprint

at least so far
I've remembered my socks and jockey shorts

the courtship of pet woman

crawling in bed with you
poses many hairy challenges

your cat sleeps between your legs
cuddling and possessive
foreplay with claws

so I move upward to your lips
your dog licks my face
friendly and hungry for attention

I coax them off the bed
and reach out to you
whatcha gonna do with that horse?

the game

it was a larger moment
that balanced the disappointment
for a second-string Buddha
who never learned to play the game
a moment unlike this world
where even an orgasm
is virally infected

where the difference
between queen and whore
is tone of voice
where men pray
our mind goes
before our penis

where people sleep with anyone
but never awaken with them
and our soul mates
once they understand us
leave

where that larger moment captured me
during a game of backgammon
"You're cheating," I chuckled
"I didn't know there were rules," she smiled

the ending

he said:
"I'm not the puppydog you think I am"

she said, with irony in her voice:
"I know you're not"

she said:
"Having sex with another man is no big deal"

he said, with bitterness in his voice:
"I know it's not"

searching

as we embrace
she looks at me
with searching eyes
and asks
"Do you own your home,
or do you rent?"

a girl's best friend

I've heard
that De Beers
has perfected a process
to turn cow shit into diamonds
to be used in computers

it all comes together you know
people and computers
I've watched women
follow diamonds
into cow shit
for years

old girlfriends

my old girlfriends
routinely change
their dreams
their men
their colors
like chameleons
trying on new roles
worshipping at the mirror
of their unfocused selves

substituting diets and makeup
for inward reflection
judging others
to keep their emptiness at bay

like Bukowski, I give them
to all the men
who seek them

the revenge brigade

beware men!
the revenge brigade is marching

they want you
to pay for your forefathers' sins

fair trade
foreskin for forefather

balls on the half shell
it's open season, men

the sensitive ones will go first

much

you may not think I'm much, baby
but I'm a friend of mine
and lately I find
much
is highly overrated

yin/yang/yin

there is a
female silence
that responds
to a male monologue
that makes no connection

he doesn't want to know
what lies within her heart
but only wants her body
her compliance
and cannot hear
her silent scream

when later she meets
a man who cares
and could understand
it remains withheld
as she offers
her body instead

if you listen
you can hear his scream
the gentlest of men
like the gentlest of women
break

emotionally broke

I'm so broke
honey

I can't even
spend
the night

the trick

as my love for her deepens
a sad discovery jolts me
she is emotionally limited

"Let me carry your burden," I say
ah, such ego always goes unrewarded
"You taught me how to feel,"
she says, lingering
for a few timeless moments

now she's "feeling" someone else
shattering my illusions like a broken mirror
the trick is not to become bitter
to know the dream doesn't fail
only the choice

vulnerable

I want
a woman
who understands
that someone
I accidentally
mesmerize
will destroy me

small fish and spider webs

love's rain beats down so hard
small fish drift into spider webs
the sky is a glowing gray vagina
which pulls me into clouds
and rains me back to earth
the glow graces my life
and frames my journey's end

I reach out for love
I have tried to learn from women
they have destroyed me
and brought me back to life
sometimes I can change it
sometimes it changes me

I cannot direct it
it creates its own pattern
and spins its own endings
as I drift between the raindrops
swimming the glowing gray sky
watching love draw me into webs
from which I cannot drift

locks

love is a transitory thing
creeping out the door
just when you think it's there to stay

fear of the slamming door
causes one to build locks, to keep emotion out
love has a key, though, that makes no noise in the lock
creeping in any hour of the day or night

I've long since quit locking doors
when they open I'm ready
for the pleasure and eventual sadness
that inevitably comes

locks are no answer
one day you'd lock the door
to find happiness has passed you by
at least they won't say I haven't tried

hell

I meet you
for the first time
after looking for you
for decades

discover
as my breath catches inside my chest
that you were just leaving
where I was heading

that, my love
is hell

part III - uneven path

shrink

during my internship as
a marriage and family therapist
my fees are determined
by a client's income

a prostitute who is
seeing me around sexual
abuse issues decides
to change her profession
to retrain as a secretary

she jokes that her
shrink's fees shrunk
in direct proportion to
her growth

a cultural event

one night I heard an offer
on late night TV
a new credit card with
no deposit required
designed to establish credit

when you need it
it's good for $500 bail
a cultural event
banks have targeted
a whole new population
for a get-out-of-jail card

out of the box

once
I bought
a word processor
thinking my '50s typewriter
took too much time

two years later
I sold it
still in the box
advertising it
as
a virgin

which I also
never really
wanted

dinosaurs

dinosaurs
pterodactyls
mastodons
Ronald Reagan
Bette Davis
your mother's love
the British royal family
J. Edgar Hoover
Richard Nixon
your father's guidance
idealism
self-respect
the perfect lover
tenderness
honesty
a free lunch
childhood heroes
fairy tale dreams
all gone

madness

Sartre was a speed freak
Ben Franklin a letch
George Washington fooled around on Martha
Beethoven was a drunkard
J.F.K. screwed Marilyn Monroe
and I get depressed
Maybe it's the madness that saves us

buk

reversing the sleeping order
he lived by night
using drink
to slow down the film
to examine each frame
revealing childhood scars
and a life of numbing injury
in a whisper louder than words

restlessly rambling

restlessly rambling
a timeless plane
a hunter stalks
his own blood-spoor

while pursuing finite answers
ripping his jugular
spurting self-hatred
unreachable perfection search

silently the hunted turns
listening to the singing of the plane
that during the endless pursuit
has merged with hunted and hunter

and the hunter becomes the hunted
becomes the plane
timelessly finding the answer - no answer
the ending - the beginning

hooked

Errol Flynn
as a young boy
learned ducks couldn't digest pork

he fed one some
concealed on a hook
attached to a fishing line

watching it pass
through the duck
feeding it to still another duck

and so on
until the whole flock was strung together
a quacking necklace

unlike ducks
we eat pride
passing it on
to brothers and sisters
of the string

tonsils kissing tail feathers
popinjays on a hook
wrapped in undigested dreams
delivered to heartbreak kitchen
smeared on stale crackers
pride de foie gras

upended

my uncle Richard
smoked a pipe
for fifty years
dangled
from the right side
of his mouth
until he developed
cancer

a corner of the lip
was replacèd
by skin
from his rear end
looking so natural
you couldn't tell
the difference
except for a slight drool

he had become
the only man I knew
who could kiss
his own behind

cognitivis interruptus

freeform days are passing
into one-dimensional constrictions
of starving prophylactic selves
covering souls like condoms

interrupting joyful primal yarp
that dances between our legs
caressing our hearts
joyfully exploding in our minds

cognitivis interruptus
covers our souls with latex straitjackets
absence of feeling numbing our minds
paralyzing our journey
devouring all tenderness
leaving us dreaming of unsheathed moments

hell is a pigeon with an attitude

hell doesn't scream
it coos silent judgments

not good enough
not good enough

not good enough son
not good enough parent
not good enough moneymaker—
the making of which often defines
not good enough lover
as judgmental crows croak

not good enough
not good enough

not good enough dreams
not good enough reality
not good enough lobotomy
murmuring and squawking

not good enough
not good enough

until I realize
following dogma
will never be enough
as the crow's compulsive caw
exposes a pigeon
with an attitude

ugly

A very fat man
with grossly disfigured face
from the Vietnam war
preaches
on fundamentalist TV

bragging he's a Victorian nerd
yelling guilt-ridden values
he mocks:
"Y'all know that's sick
but y'all pray for me
I have braimdanage."

his circus act drones on
with no love or soul
show biz or dogma
turning guilt into money

I muttered:
"Inside and out, baby,
you're one ugly motherfucker."

perhaps

perhaps you're different
it's not a sin you know
although you may have heard otherwise

maybe the purpose of existence
is to be who you goddamn want

the ant and the grasshopper revisited
or deferred gratification sucks
or play misty for me

Anal the ant
spent his days and nights
collecting grapes
preparing for winter
for a rainy day
for unforeseen events
hauling, sweating, groaning
pushing ever harder
against a heartless world

Misty, his wife
cleaned the house
cooked the food
washed the clothes
waiting patiently for Anal
to come to bed

but Anal never came
growing bent and early old
he'd fall next to Misty
instantly asleep
as Misty breathed heavily

one morning
Happy Dick, the grasshopper
drifted past Anal's house
fiddling a happy tune
in time with Anal's labors
"Let's celebrate the moment,"
he smiled

Anal only grunted
pushing Misty back inside
to resume her duties
as she frowned
hoping for better days

winter came
not Anal
who died of exhaustion
Happy Dick chirped his condolences,
under the loving sky that embraced them
in the beauty of the moment
morning came
finding Misty sighing quite another sigh
as they fiddled each other
and nibbled on Anal's grapes

which leaves this moral
he who works and never plays
does not come but goes

calling delbara

calling my friend Vasily
can be an exercise in futility
because his wife Delbara
newly arrived from Ukraine
always answers the phone

understanding no English
she mutters her discontent
will not give him the phone
I finally hang up
as she growls her frustration
because she isn't done
not understanding

Vasily's message never arrives
its content lost and distorted
explaining it later to Vasily
he doesn't understand
and says, smiling,
"No problem, no problem"

I grin, give him a hug
pour the vodka
that, we both understand

blues

Etta James,
her early fame forgotten
appearing at the Rainbow tavern
world weary, middle-aged
survivor

surrounded by a roomful of
aging women
who lovingly enfold her
she squats
as if to take a shit

the room suddenly silent
she sings
the been fucked over
used to be addicted
don't give a damn
'bout how you see me baby

best damn voice I ever heard

blues

going, going, gone

my wife and I join another couple
for a night on the town in Tokyo

ducking out of the rain
we find a brightly lit nightclub
where couples are dancing
to American rock 'n' roll

are immediately collected
by a seven-foot Japanese bouncer
who says we can only dance
with "house girls"

leads us to a second level
with circular seating
overlooking the dance floor
we drink and watch

women of grace and beauty
join men at their tables
each wearing a device
allowing them to be tracked
on a large computer screen
in a back room
each table paying by the minute
for their company

the third tier has rooms
designed for more private moments
after the men leave, bouncers
probe panties and bras for concealed tips

I shout over my drink
"It's a computerized whore house!"

two dignified Japanese men approach us
thinking my wife a house girl
they politely offer
to buy her services

she grabs my hand to leave when
I start the bidding at
ten thousand American dollars

american gangsters

my wife and I have breakfast
in a Hong Kong hotel coffee shop
on the Kowloon side of the bay

two friends burst victoriously
into the cafe, one waving
a Rolex watch
"Look, it's solid gold,
　at one quarter of the retail price!"

examining it, I comment
"The watchband is stamped Y.G."
he turns pale
"Shit! Y.G. means gold plated.
Those sons of bitches!
Kowloon shops have a no-return policy."

I respond "Around here
Americans are seen either
as bumbling fools
or fugitives from an old
gangster movie.
Let's have a little fun and
change the policy.
You do your Bogart imitation,
I'll do Cagney."

we enter the shop
our wives wait, frightened, outside
two clerks and the owner
nervously watch us enter
each of us with one hand
in pants pocket

a clerk attempts
to duck behind a counter
"Everyone put your hands
on the counter now!"
screams Cagney

Bogart demands exchange for purchase price
minus five dollars
allowing the owner to save face
Bogart and Cagney back out slowly
hands still in pockets

late that night in a hotel bar
Bogart lisps to Cagney
"They won't believe this at home."
Cagney shrugs
pours another drink

in defense of a loving ecology

you act
like you're the only damned person
on the planet earth

you took it all
for you
and left nothing for me

workout at fifty

exercise machines
clank rhythmically
rock video playing in the background
four sultry women
singing "you're never gonna get it"

a desperation lingers
hanging in the air
it's not that exercise
isn't good
it's the compulsion
to stay young, unchanged

a young woman
presses more weight than me
gaunt features, perfect body
muscle, sinew, and bone
no softness
youth without sensuousness

her determined expression
echoes the video
"you're never gonna get it"
I don't want it
or these sore ligaments
or this compulsive battle with time

give me a bottle of wine
my aging body
a sensuous, softer woman
more my age
with velvety body and spirit
where muscle, sinew, and bone

have embraced a more genial result
who sings
"we're both gonna get it, baby—
not at the health club, either"

single man's shopping list at middle age

Epson salt
Dr. Scholl's foot pads
lens cleaner
vodka
coffee
aspirin
K-Y Jelly
condoms
lottery tickets
oh yeah - food

downward development

just bought a bottle
of 4.99 wine
not great but it'll do
saves me ten bucks a bottle
amazing how "it'll do"
turns into
"good shit"

one screaming morning

I barely remember
to put towels in the dryer
muttering to myself
"got to keep it together"

a small voice
deep inside
whispers quietly
It's all right, baby
barely keeping it together
counts.

leaves and water

in my back yard
sits a weathered flower pot
white with two minotaur heads
on either side of a crack
that dribbles leaves and water
collected from a storm

it once belonged to a lover
who abandoned me
a chipped clay token
which has become dead leaves
floating in murky water
like the memory
of long departed love

funky leather pouch

funky leather pouch of my mind
smelling of earthy tobacco
well-smoked memories
erasing themselves as they happen

the fit

I push back
stretch
growl joyful noise
wallow
in my well-worn
leather reclining chair

there was a time
its size overwhelmed me
now
like life
I've grown into it

the dance

a man in my neighborhood
plays a drum duet
with a passing ice cream truck

blending drum rolls
and rim shots
to the music of the Sundance Kid

as children do quarter skips
in time
with melting ice cream dreams

green

the hedge you chopped to smithereens
is greening nicely now

too bad your newly painted
baby blue house
and your newly built
chainlink fence
can't follow suit

boring

"Why'd you pull
me over officer?

I wasn't speeding
or on drugs
don't get drunk
anymore

I'm good to
my wife
kind to animals
courteous to
strangers"

he wrote me
a ticket
for being boring

two alley cats

looking out my front window
I see my neighbor looking back at me
we survey our territory
like two alley cats

he smiles and nods
I smile and nod
each thinking "get the hell out of my view"
he told me the other day he is moving

I wished him well
when his moving van has left
I will walk across the street
and pee on his front porch

part IV - breaking the surface

flowers and children

outside
you can see
both flowers and children bloom

my child runs to greet me
the first time in a week
she grows so beautiful

come visit me, my little flower
run across the grass, laughing
I smile with you

your young girl chatty words
your wise silence, older than your years
dancing all around on your gentle way

midnight

I sit alone by the fire
wood fragments burning slowly
brightening the calm of midnight

forty years have burned away
as I once again explore
a life so long deferred

I hear the muffled sound
of rain caressing the earth
tapping at my roof, playing with the silence

I seek peace
begin to write a poem in time
to the rhythm of the rain

my fireplace thickens with cold ashes
embers burned from orange to gray
loneliness and the night are only half over

like an old monk in a dark robe I sit alone
tomorrow my child comes to play
her vibrant bloom, my legacy, will bring a new day

me next

my poems breathe
like dozens of story children
fidgeting inside
pleading
"me, me
me next, Daddy."

some days they nap
other times I can't write
fast enough
to push them all
through the birth canal

during these moments
unable to get it all down
my pen leaves
a different kind
of stretch mark

children

my poems
are my children

sometimes more so
than my real child

they don't tell me
I didn't write them

charles bukowski

though dead
he shines more alive
than most living
asking to be regarded
as nothing

seeking in death
peace absent in life
his spirit drinks wine
laughing at us
who grieve his passing

hard red

Red owns an L.A. bookstore
sells signed first editions
was friend of Charles Bukowski
who wrote of Red's impatience
with those who only came to browse

he growls short answers to my questions
he thinks a waste of time
I call him some years later
to buy Bukowski from afar
he softens on the phone
"It's okay kid, don't worry
I'll hold the books till you can pay."
when I call today
his words conceal a fragile edge
"Hurry up and buy the books kid
I won't be around much longer."

my throat lumps
first Bukowski, now Red
when he leaves I'll weep
for him, for Bukowski, for me
Red might say
"Pull yourself together kid."
it's all so simple
but I know simple
is one definition of hard

the clotting

in our blind struggle
imperfections cut our feet
like shards of glass

it's only blood though
evaporating into rosy mist
heartaches, hopes and fear
merging into crimson sun

the past matters not
life is a transformational blood clot
fading into tearful mist

drifting upwards through time
like a loving sigh
breathing into forever
listen, you can hear it whisper

the kiss

I kissed her thinking of forever
as she kissed my ass goodbye

the years unveiled a chronic yearning
that lurked within me all along

groaning, growling, ever present
a void of such intense proportions

gnawing into half my soul
but the other half remaining

stretched and grew
to make me whole

so when embracing new forevers
I don't forget and lose my soul

reprieve

a growling windstorm
rips and gashes through trees
gulping and gnawing my yard
wood fragments crashing everywhere
a runaway fir smashes through a fence
pounding the yard next door

it could have demolished my house
or two others
but landing opposite the wind's direction
a reprieve is granted
until next time

i don't have the heart

walking out on the deck
I see a tiny chipmunk.
brown with black stripes
five inches long
chowing down in the bird feeder

grabbing a squirt gun
reserved for larger gray squirrels
who dominate the feeder
daring me to chase them away,
I shoot

the chipmunk looks at me, shocked
"Why are you bothering me?
Generations of us have fed off spilled birdseed
that has fallen to the deck."

but taking over the feeder—
that's going too far—
I see they've gnawed a tunnel
through a deck board
opening to the supports below
probably a nest

he ambles across the railing
stops and stares at me
I blast him again
shaking himself he jumps
fifteen feet to the woods below

leaving his mate sunning herself on the deck
looking very pregnant
watching me in disgust
she peers over the edge

"You're not going to make me
jump, too, are you--asshole!"

I zap her
glaring at me she hesitates
then steps off the deck
heavily dropping into the foliage below

I feel like shit
watch for them all week
when he reappears I let him be

yesterday both of them
were lounging in the bird feeder
to my relief she's okay
watching them sleep in the feeder
paws and tails hanging over the edge
I just don't have the heart

smile

removing braces after three years
for jaw pain
I find relief
and surprisingly straighter teeth

my orthodontist says,
"Bleaching them will make you look
like a movie star."

watching my reflection
relaxing tight-lipped Bogart smile
that hid the latticework

I know whiter-than-life
smiles mean more
to my orthodontist
than to me

birthing

flashing neck pain
jerks me awake
last night's carousing
once again triggering old injuries

an orthopedic surgeon
seats me in his office
leaves to process x-rays

I hear commotion
step into the hall
watch several nurses stare
in disbelief
at x-rays on a bulletin board

one says "My god,
this isn't possible!"
"It's one for the medical journals,"
says another
"Those are mine!"
they scatter in embarrassment

the doctor returns
"At birth your lower neck
contained two fused vertebrae.
The spinal cord was forced to grow outside the bone
a rare form of spina-bifida.
It should have caused your respiratory system to fail.
How you lived is unexplainable.
Apparently in time
bone closed around the cord.
You've damaged that area before.
Unfortunately yesterday's injury affects this region—
there's nothing we can do."

in a daze, one hand on
aching neck, I return home
how would knowing this earlier
have affected my being?
would I have avoided risk?
been afraid to damage
the delicate balance

had fewer car wrecks?
drunk thousands of gallons
of wine less to kill the pain?
chosen not to fuck
in precarious positions?
sidestepped life's darker side?

I would surely have
avoided military service in the reserves
to escape Vietnam
could have chosen a different road
offering fewer jolts to
body and soul
I could have become
boring—

exploring further I visit
a rebirther
teacher of reverse breathing
enabling me to relive
the moment of my birth

I am pure energy
pushing hard
against a wall of solid bone
struggling to arrive

returning to the present
I sadly understand
how I've pursued my dreams
straining, struggling
instinctively fearing for my life
willfulness pushing against bone

brushing away tears
I begin
the long lonely journey
to balance my
intensity

the voice within

my grieving moves
into a moment of grace
reviving my confidence
softening a journey through my darker side

gently nudging aside
the deathly remains
of rejected love's searing pain
as a cherished heart forever closes itself to me

a surge of grief
attempts to blow me away
a voice within me urges
do not surrender but seek peace

the mournful storm slows
powerless against the enduring earth
it will soon subside
as my heart rejoins my soul

whiplash

once upon a time
a whiplash of financial insecurity
led me to work in business
helping executives put bandaids
on corporate symptoms

but an emptiness persisted
a yearning
for love and transformation
which I had abandoned
in my fear

I learned
there are worse things
than financial instability
or fear of persecution
or persecution

there is the void
created by neglecting
my heart's desire
the primal spiritual pull
toward completion

which never-endingly
whispers
Embrace
what you can't control.
Let love do the rest.

painless

a friend once
asked me to co-author
a how-to book
about how to transform
without pain

halfway through the book
I realized I didn't know
how to do that
he said "write it anyway,
it'll sell"

withdrawing from the project
I realized
I had learned something

for bob

the polluted sky
turns
foggy blue
melting into empty
like us
my friend

empty's not so bad
you know
I ache
to not be contained
in the empty
between planes

to float away
to loose the silver chord
that holds me
to this body
to earth

could I but fly
ever upward
moving freely
not returning

oh my friend
with limited time
could I but
trade places with
you

so you could
bask in the love
of your beautiful
family

and I could
transcend this loneliness

I love you
and know
when you break free
we will meet again

aroused erotic chair

the gallery is alive
curious people intently viewing
the Zen paintings and sculpture
of Richard Kirsten Daiensai
loving energy emanates from his paintings

after seventy years the artist/priest
still exudes passion
joyfully welcoming everyone
especially the women
who relish his erotic interplay
between senses and spirit

escaping the intensity of the crowd
I duck into a side room
slump into an antique chair
an upwelling of sensuous energy
rushes through my body
my ears ring
feelings of joy, well being
wash sweetly over me

Daiensai must have recently
meditated in the chair
I motion to a friend
"You have to sit in this chair,
 the energy will make love to you."
"I don't feel anything," she teases
"You must have soaked it up."

Daiensai watches grinning
later we talk as I buy a painting
feels like reuniting with an old friend

his eyes twinkle, "When I
return from Japan
I'll have a surprise for you."

six months later
I walk into the gallery
spotting me he laughs
"I've been waiting for you.
It's somewhere in the back room;
find it and it's yours."

sorting through stacks of lithographs
I discover the image of a chair
suspended in time
penis rising
pointing to an orb of light

the captured moment of my
basking in Daiensai's delicious energy
transformed into a humorous Zen image

laughing with him I rejoice
in another human being
celebrating lightly the joy
of sensuality moving into spirituality

garden party

in the garden of my wife's
friend's daughter after the wedding
the tearful mother fears the groom's
family will steal her daughter

I leave my wife to
comfort the mother of the bride
approach the groom's mother who is
stone-faced and pale

helpfully suggest that maybe a couple
comes together to learn something from
each other which neither family has chosen
she says "Maybe so"

hugging the groom's mother I
begin to search for several glasses of wine
but am instead ambushed by a
twitchy red-eyed little man who
has just performed the marriage

he invites me to join other
twitchy men who are discussing Henry Miller
we stand in a circle like
little boys comparing our pee-pees

"Miller was an expatriate" says red eyes
"he saw the U.S. for what it really was"
shit, I think, I did this already
attempt to move closer to the wine

I say to the pee-pees
"he wrote like a poet
when it works his metaphor moves
freely through streams of primal irreverence that

inspires my writing, but his early writing
contains very little love"

red eyes frowns like I'd just
peed on his shoes which suddenly
doesn't seem like a bad idea
instead I leave the preacher to
pee on his own shoes, drawn
by the blooping of a tuba

I watch the groom's father stiffly
dancing with my wife to the
jangled sounds of a bad Dixieland band
her sparkling oval eyes embrace me
we share a smile as someone
taps my shoulder

a young woman from the neighborhood
who didn't attend the wedding purrs
"sit by me"
I watch her sad-eyed husband
attend their two small daughters

"I'm only back in my marriage
for the summer"
she confides awaiting my response
"Excuse me," I mumble setting out
to reclaim my wife who is
comforting the mother
of the mother of the bride
because she isn't the center of attention

I bring them
two pieces of wedding cake
and set the scene for our escape

beverly hills reading

after a reading
of passionate love poetry
a woman of eighty
approached me

fearing she was offended
I braced myself
but found her
open, beautiful and bright

she hugged me
expressing her joy
at sensuality moving into spirituality

that day
one of my biases
disappeared forever

i hear you cry

I hear you cry
but can't aid you
beautiful sister

I sense your pain
and can't change your reality

I share mine
hoping it useful
don't ask me to change you
beautiful sister

hate my honesty
find solace in my pain

thanks guys

Walt Whitman
Charles Bukowski
Raymond Carver
shared pathos
wonder
a middle-aged erection

their playgrounds were different
but their dance
cleared ever more paths
in this uptight world
for people like
me

if i could cast a shadow

if I could cast a shadow
that included the lure
of the world I love

I would feel my life complete
and could let go that shadow
and watch it soften and flow
into the essence of others

gentle breezes

you are truly beautiful
and need control
as you struggle with your life

I gave up
my need for love
accepting what was offered

tossing away years of knowledge
drifting within your charms
hoping for what could later come

but later never came
leaving us gut-empty
and hungry for gentle breezes

reluctantly I discovered
we cannot create a tragedy
and expect a happy ending

sitting

sitting, drinking wine
on a deck hanging over
a stream that rushes
down a green ravine

that surrounds all—
birds, stream, and me

down the ravine wafts
the smell of a far-off barbecue
as I feel the sunlight
bathe us

emerging shadows dance
through towering trees
under steel blue sky

moment becomes feeling
feeling becomes presence
tender, sensual—All
earth   universe   me

making soup

celebrating the millennium
I brew a pot of hearty soup
thickened
with split-pea memories
blended with ham-chunk dreams
sprinkled
with the pepper of my passion
combined in rich love broth

I'll fill my bowl, devour it
return for seconds then thirds
pause to consider conventional
wisdom
that proclaims the reaching
for a fourth bowl
not the smartest choice

I hear myself mutter
"conventional wisdom is highly overrated"
ignores a richer understanding
condemns
a more sensual way

so I'll focus on the magic
created through my feelings
embrace the heartfelt gifts
concealed within the mix
I'll proceed with sweet abandon
stride right up to the pot
for my glorious fourth helping
God, I love pea soup!

part V - fresh dawn

longing

I long to walk with another who has
left the world far behind
but no one comes

I long to laugh with another who has
left the world far behind
but no one comes

I long to love with another who has
left the world far behind
but no one comes

I long to cry with another who has
left the world far behind
but no one comes

let's jump

let's jump
through a crack in the sidewalk
together

flawlessness
leaves us nothing
to give the other
but silence

the search

a bloody-mary sun
once again sets
straining through the terraced black circles
of my eyes

I seek you
in all the wrong places
bumping into hard edges
that are not you

I mistake vagina for soul
such a sad delusion
the foreplay of broken promises

searching for you
walking crowded streets
peering into passing cars
wandering grocery stores, art galleries, bookstores

probing the laughter of children
sniffing the gentle wind
hearing the sigh of god
lying in the arms of the wounded

drowning in wine bottles
walking ocean beaches
crying out in dreams
staring into the soulless eyes of strangers

fondling store window mannequins
drifting past alcoholic slaughterhouses
falling into a young mother's eyes
as she proudly walks her baby down the lane
pointing out the universe

embracing self-centered lovers,
offering noble-sounding excuses
for their thoughtlessness

through this madness comes a whisper
soul seeks that which is like itself
embrace vulnerability and tenderness
let go control and look within—

finally you appear
honest, open, caring, whole
beautiful and sensuous
with no hard edges

tears stream down my face
I cry "where the hell have you been?"
you smile, hold my head to your breast

as the bloody sun turns to gold
darkness disappearing from my eyes
our souls blend in trust
flow into love's remembered light

uneven burning

as he shoved a log
into his fireplace
he shoved it in crooked
out of balance
which caused the fire to burn unevenly

leaving a sculpture
of freedom
which begged to be seen
by a woman
who was searching for a man
who didn't need to be
perfect
to touch god

moon shift

we dance
in crazy wild circles
hungry for the promise
that each fulfills the other

my hand caresses the nipple of your breast
two fingers slipping between your legs
where you're wet

you close your eyes
and caress my genitals
dreaming of love

as we pass one another
in opposite directions
trapped in our desire for safety

my dreams fall to earth
in crumpled heaps
you are surprised

I don't know how to tell you
I have never been loved enough
and the quarter moon sinks
behind the collecting clouds

I fear one quarter is all I'll ever know
unlock the door to my dark, love
light the way

how can I tell you my regrets
how can I speak my shame at being abandoned
when I have never spoken it before

how should I approach you
with my strength and passion
or with tear stained sobs

I take off my clothes
and walk across the room
the path is uneven

I stand before you a long time
should I sing or cry
I no longer know the difference

you snuggle in my arms
I fear you don't understand
though you know enough of love
to look at me
and tell me that you do

I cover your loins with kisses
each kiss a wish
a bouquet from my heart
in danger of being torn to pieces

please take my hand
lead me to your love
loving each other
is all we have left

but which of us is strong enough
to peel petals from the bouquet
and fling them upwards
letting go our control

they will not fall to earth
but will remain
suspended in time
food for the moon
with the prayer it will become full

silent rhythm

a quiet rhythm flows
through your bell-like silence
penetrating my restless being
with a caution that rings true

our bell towers are not unalike
your rhythm reaches
so deeply within
we breathe together

love me

I sit quietly, listening to
falling leaves
lonely, my past faded
my sleeve wet with tears

the tears have stopped
my mind is clear
decades divide us
but we have loved many lifetimes

love me

looking up I see the rising sun
unbearable loneliness
I clutch my robe and lean
against the empty window

love me

I have had too much to drink
my feeling for you crests
our ages deny our future
yet our love is real

love me

we will return to our paths
our dreams will move us
over our individual fields and mountains
what is there to think about

what is there to doubt
we have enduring love
we have now

soul mates

you are the brakes
my love
to my 16-valve, 4-cylinder
engine

reaching out to me
as we round the
curve

your caution lingers
as I put my foot to the floor
balancing me
enabling us both
to round the curve

we can't make it
without the other
you wouldn't approach
the curve
and I wouldn't
finish it

love with a cold

you can rub your drippy nose
all over my body

and I'll drip over you
in another way

instead of the marathon
I had in mind
we'll share tenderness

that's how I feel about you
anyway

the softening

I awaken groaning
searing neck pain
charley horse clutching my leg
shaking it off
head in hand
inching out of bed
hoping moving around
will ease the pain

drinking fresh coffee
hand still on neck
I read a Bukowski poem
about a cat
with back broken
again and again
who, like Bukowski
endures

softly my lady rises
touching me with healing hands
love flowing through her
into my neck
she asks me to envision
spaces between the concrete
that surround the pain

as stiffness eases
she caresses me with light
and asks
"is there anything else you want?"
"I have it all" I whisper
she kisses my neck
my face

sighing, I feel
in ways
I never could have dreamed

rich

thirty years ago a
psychic told me in
the presence of my wife
that my second wife
would have white hair
and be wealthy

sitting here with my
white-haired second wife
I joyfully observe her
spiritual wealth and
await, grinning, for her
to win the lottery

freeway to ahhhh

hey
I've found a highway
that leads away from this empty place

I don't belong here
and could always come back
if I want to

it's time to drop my training wheels
to live my dreams
I leave behind cleverness
it kills the soul, you know

I've seen people die of genius
I strip down
not only to flesh
but to soul

I will find someone
who chooses not to just flirt with love
I sense her tender soul

smell her sweetness
nuzzle the softness of her skin
taste her delicately sensual mouth
get lost in the fluidity of her hips

as she dances into her dreams
flesh moving into purity
as we sail along the loving freeway
to ahhhh

see the ocean

see the ocean rise and fall
it will rise and fall again
as we cast a restless shadow
in a tidal afterglow

let us climb the crest together
and leave this much behind
watch the ocean rise and fall
and rise and fall again

safe

my love
you have given me
something
not even my mother gave

the gift
of feeling safe
in a woman's arms

kiss yourself

as I kissed my love
she whispered you have great lips

not as sweet as yours, I said
if you haven't kissed yourself
how would you know, she laughed

I guess I've only done it
symbolically
and the times I did
have been too embarrassing
to admit

there's a poem, she smiled

my farewell

weaving heartaches into love
I vacuumed my farewell
to living womb that held my changes
through healing years in green-tree grove
a birthing spirit needing weaning
embraced by those who went before

I could hear the vacuum singing
mournful humming bluesy wail
as electric light-filled voices
echoed plaintive bagpipe moan
that sang goodbye to tearful sorrow
aching struggles in the night

soon a soul more freshly wounded
comes to rest in love's retreat
to take her turn in the embracing
the gentle presence of the light

I leave to join a tender soul mate
to dance with spirit in the spaces
where all-surrounding forest rises
high above a rushing stream

throughout my journey I'll remember
when mystic spirits of the grove
held me through my darkest moments
till I could learn to love myself

walking together

I look back upon
the many adventures of
my life, the risks
taken, the thin
edge I have walked
creating many lives within
the illusion of this one

today I have to smile
celebrating what I have
found
with you, my love

I remember the image
of a poster depicting
a little boy walking with
a little girl, holding hands

I imagine the two of us
walking down that path
you encouraging
"come on Jimmie"
to my hesitant "okaaay"

as we walk together
my heart tells me
that where we are going
is less important
than who we are with

part VI - toward the horizon

the glowing

each morning
I awaken
make coffee
cross the road
in front of my home
for the morning paper
road on one side
ravine, stream and forest
on the other

carefully moving back
avoiding morning traffic
I shift
away from a rushing world
into the glowing

it peeks between trees
reflects from luminous throats
of hummingbirds
shimmers
against a rushing stream
dances in morning fog
rising ghostlike
from the forest floor
becomes lacy white light
washing over everything
and me

having stepped back
across the road
I realize
how easily
the glowing disappears
when I lose myself
in an accelerated world

old bones and long grass

I feel the chill of an old wind
the breeze knows when to come
softly motioning to my spirit
whispering of the journey ahead

a ghost runs loose in the long grass
its sigh stretches to heaven
I hear singing, I know it's me
the ghost smiles and beckons

rock me awake, sweet spirit
speak to me, thou frosty beard
I've been asleep in the weeds
locked in decay and old bones

now the wind is at my back
the sky has cracked open
the world I knew shifted ninety degrees
the ghost moves closer

I'm awake all over
having moved through the stony night
basking in the long grass
as the spirit wind caresses my genitals

yesterday I nearly whispered myself away
sleeping the sleep old bones know
today is warmed by changing visions
that radiate loving flashes of light-song

transform me, my ghostly friend
loosen my brittle ways
we've met before, I remember now
we never enter the long grass alone

I see my father's stoic smile
I hear my grandfather's throaty chuckle
their son, the composite of many fathers,
yearns to be a brother

the loving presence moves, yet remains
playing my spirit like a tenor guitar
making music from white light
leaving me unafraid and singing in the long grass

inspired by Theodore Roethke

dreams

dreams are tools of sublimated madness
where everyday appearances reveal surreal images

the dreamer emerges from the clouds
transcending the vision

reawakening into new reality
inviting dialogue with one's former self

risking dissonance with one's friends
perhaps with one's former life

heavy is the price to pass beyond the mirror
resounding the transformation

swollen birds

bleeding stars
birds falling from a blown-out sky
swollen with misdirection
their rotted eyes reflecting a ravaged dream
of free flight

they sing sorrow and pain
lamenting the poisoning of our spirit
vacant unfinished dreams
where once was longing

so this is death
this absence of pain or joy
or any other feeling but despair

directionless swimmers flounder in dry lake beds
where living the passion we were born with is a crime
the purity of birth is replaced
by swollen egos, pregnant with dead dreams
giving birth to stones

voices scream in the dark
as a slipstream of disappointment haunts the night
ripping and feeding on hollow dreams
where the highest fulfillment is to die
to be swallowed in cleansing earthquake
to be purified by fire

may the demon wind swallow the darkness—
seeking purification I raise a bottle to my lips
I dream of a world free to be as we were born
free to live and feel passion
to risk and have love's thirst quenched

free to write new legends
to love and transform
to pump the poison out of the ocean of our discontent
free to form a world where one does not drown in
emptiness

let the wind of change become a gale
exuding life into dead eyes
let the dead attend the dead
let the living, finally, fly free

time machine

stepping off of sadness sidewalk
cutting loose my problem shoes
floating, stumbling, running barefoot
had to lose those city-tunnel blues

stumbling on a priest of sorrow
we passed a smile, shared a toke
concealing fears about tomorrow
laughed and shared life's hollow joke

I chanced upon a time machine
with a warning flashing there
come on in, you won't return
and soon shall cease to care

just a superstition muttered I
as I staggered on within
I've had enough of sadness, sorrow
and petty sidewalk sin

so I soared above the cities
far beyond the smokey glow
to a pile of whitewashed rubble
a melted dream called future's show

below were remnants of the cities
once green meadows turned to stone
broken statues, splintered sidewalks
people's dreams in textured bone

hatred's folly spawned its own
dreams lay shattered, scattered bare
crowded sidewalks, a no-parking zone
nothing moving, no one left to care

I cried aloud, is this our fate
can we change, we have to try
throw off our bondage, abandon hate
hard to cope, I couldn't even cry

and time collapsed in rhythm
as I found myself back home
crying, laughing, ever grateful
at this chance to find my own

so now I share my journey
to all who wander near
risking laughter, sneers and slander
I sing to all who hear

cast away your earthen shadows
and seek a loving touch
come and wash away your teardrops
resume the journey, break your crutch

raise your spirits, fly beyond
redefine your changing needs
come and try to share your feelings
reap the harvest of those seeds

not coincidence

my grandfather John
accepted no limits
was curious if life
existed after death
told a friend he'd return
if he could
to share what he'd found
over there

years after his death
I'd sense his presence
especially in times of peril
once a psychic friend
spoke with John
who said, in his rasping voice
he'd stayed around
to protect me from men
but forgot
to protect me from women
you could hear his throaty chuckle

as I write this
a neighbor's dog is
singing, not howling
not coincidence
John, I feel you
in his song

soul harvest

there is room within room
spaces bordering spaces
opportunity rising through the chaos of change

life is a Mona Lisa smile
that awakens from one dream
and drifts into another

transitions turning wind lingers
I listen to the falling leaves
letting go of my control
continuing my journey, quietly expanding

sharing my journey, I walk past unfamiliar streets
as something of myself
smiles through a stranger's eyes
while helping kindred spirits
climb out of rotating pits
of circularly competitive acceptance-go-round

our heartbeat hitchhikes
across the borders of our imagination
like the hands of a flying clock
that melt into swans and crows
while life goes on all around us

we walk a short distance
but leave the world hundreds of miles away
reaping a soul harvest of changing needs

the smell of the earth
thrusts my thinking beyond my goals
transforming me into a single thought

and the trees blend in silent understanding
infinitely breathing, creating the moments
revealing a timeless majesty

that borders busy concrete realities
that contrast with the forever finished, unfinished
symphony
changes in my journey
free me even of freedom

and the gentle stream flows
nowhere and everywhere
with a dignity and a silent beauty
for which there are no words.

my spirit sings

I sit
hanging over space
overlooking green ravine
as crystal waters
stream
toward Puget Sound

old-growth cedar
hundreds of feet up
quivers through the caress
of translucent light

rain-like emanations
expanding downward
white light
weaving the spaces
enveloping the trees
and me

whooshing stream below
scent of flowering trees
birdsong exploding everywhere
filling my senses

through them
my spirit sings

the assembling

today I saw
a celestial mailbox
metallic sheen
reflecting graying sky
hanging there
suspended in time

awaiting a message
that is traveling
through time and space
from me to me

past, present, and future
blending into golden light
which whispers
let go your parts, my boy
they will assemble themselves

the bridge

we live in a world
of polarities
the complete and everlasting
fusion of opposites

*day and night
dark and light*

our hearts the bridge
connect them
beating with
the rhythm of duality

hold yourselves sacredly
within this rhythm
not becoming split
one person now
another person later

*day and night
dark and light*

in this world of shifting shadows
love is the connection
bringing dark to light
and day to night

gentleness

there is gentleness
that we
who have been close to death
embrace

permeating heartache
with silky glow
reminding me where I will return

till then
my heart holds the balance
between sunrise and
the other side of day

until light within
rejoins light without

afterword

As a small child I sat at my Romanian Gypsy grandfather's feet and listened as he and his cronies shared stories about their lawless years in Chicago during the Al Capone era. His advice to me was "be anything you goddamn want." Storytelling was in my blood.

My father was a career army officer so we moved often. Though I learned to adjust to different lifestyles, blended in quickly, and became an observer, part of me always felt like I was on the outside looking in. Years later, while playing and singing music, my stories turned into song. The lyrics became poetry with a blues rhythm and a gypsy outsider edge.

When as a young man I drowned in a surfing accident, an out-of-body near-death experience altered my reality. I left music and explored different career paths, each of them increasingly drawing me to further explore the nature of reality.

My primal years, later exploring years, and more recent introspective times are reflected in my writing, creating the stories of my life.

Writers who have influenced me include Charles Bukowski, Theodore Roethke, Robinson Jeffers, Lawrence Durrell, Wanda Coleman, and Jimmy Santiago Baca. Their writing is unrestricted by conventional thinking.

My friendship with Richard Kirsten Daiensai, Zen priest/painter/sculptor, has encouraged me to blend sensuality with spirituality in life and art. It has transformed my life.

With Phil Bevis's friendship and encouragement I shook off my cobwebs, awakened, and began to write and publish again. His editing improved my work. Arundel Press's beautifully designed publications of my broadsides and chapbook *Swan Dive*, are works of art. He also designed and published this book. Thank you so much, Phil.

Thanks to Annie Brulé, Rebecca Mancuso, and Geoff Wallace for their fine design, editing, and publishing skills. Thanks to Gregg Andrews for his help.

PoetsWest, including the reading at The Frye Art Museum in Seattle, *Spleen Quarterly*, along with the reading at the Rendezvous Bar/Jewel Box Theater in Seattle, *Indigenous Fiction, Spread,* and *Breathe* have published and encouraged me.

My gratitude goes to Elaine Phelps for her friendship and wholehearted support of my work. Thanks to Spencer Grendahl (my old partner in crime) for his encouragement, the Beverly Hills reading, and a lifetime of friendship. I am grateful to Maggie Morrison, Cal Kinnear, Terry Hill, Terry Hanna and Nancy Krogh, Jim Buhler, Rhonda Herl, Dick Spencer, Erika Andrews, Keith and Amy Griffin, and many others for their support and caring.

Thank you most of all to Esther, my life partner, best friend, talented editor, and keeper of my heart, to whom this book is dedicated.

James B. Moore, October 2014

index of poems by title

a cultural event, 98
a girl's best friend, 84
after dark, 23
american gangsters, 116
the ant and the grasshopper, 110
army reserve summer camp, 44
aroused erotic chair, 153
the assembling, 201
back again, 48
beverly hills reading, 157
bimbo love, 68
birthing, 145
blues, 113
boring, 129
the bridge, 202
buk, 102
bye, 70
calling debara, 112
the caress, 49
charles bukowski, 137
children, 136
the chosen, 41
cinderella and the seven dwarfs, 65
clarence, 35
the clotting, 139
the code, 28
cognitivis interruptus, 106
the courtship of pet woman, 80
crystal snifter, 75
damn yankee, 21
the dance, 127
deep, 71
dinosaurs, 100
do you love her you poor bastard, 73
don't you kill him, 67
downward development, 122
dreams, 192
emotionally broke, 89
the ending, 82
the fit, 126
five minutes, 46
flowers and children, 133
for bob, 151
freeway to ahhhh, 181
fuck and die, 60
funky leather pouch, 125
the game, 81
garden party, 155
gentle breezes, 161
the gentle wind whispers, 58
gentleness, 203
the gift, 72
the glowing, 189
going, going, gone, 114
green, 128
hanging down, 33
hard red, 138
hell, 94
hell is a pigeon with an attitude, 107
hooked, 104
the hunt, 40
i don't have the heart, 142
i hear you cry, 158
if I could cast a shadow, 160

in defense of a loving ecology, 118
interrupted journey, 61
is that all, 31
the kiss, 140
kiss yourself, 184
leaves and water, 124
let me, 56
let's jump, 168
the light bled, 69
locks, 93
longing, 167
love me, 175
love with a cold, 177
madness, 101
make it noisy, 47
making soup, 163
male bonding, 38
may i see wandell, please, 18
me next, 135
men are like dogs, 79
micelike, 45
midnight, 134
moon shift, 172
moonlight ride, 59
much, 87
my farewell, 185
my lady, 57
my spirit sings, 200
the new kid, 28
not coincidence, 197
now, 55
old bones and long grass, 190
old girlfriends, 85
one screaming morning, 123
out of the box, 99
painless, 150

performance cancelled, 29
perhaps, 109
princess bride, 76
princess leaping, 64
reflections from the hungry turtle cocktail lounge, 66
reprieve, 141
restlessly rambling, 103
the revenge brigade, 86
rich, 180
the road most traveled, 34
safe, 183
scratch, 52
the search, 169
searching, 83
see the ocean, 182
she, 63
shifted, 78
shrink, 97
silent rhythm, 174
simple wisdom, 50
single man's shopping list at middle age, 121
sitting, 162
small fish and spider webs, 92
smile, 144
snakes know, 51
the softening, 178
soul harvest, 198
soul mates, 176
swan dive, 62
swollen birds, 193
thanks guys, 159
time machine, 195
to whom it may concern, 43
train ride, 25
the trick, 90

two alley cats, 130
ugly, 108
unchained spirit, 13
uneven burning, 171
up, 74
upended, 105
the voice within, 148
vulnerable, 91
walking together, 186
whiplash, 149
workout at fifty, 119
yin/yang/yin, 88

www.ingramcontent.com/pod-product-compliance
Lightning Source LLC
Chambersburg PA
CBHW020410080526
44584CB00014B/1253